Beading

By Angela Adair

This edition published in 2012
By SpiceBox™
12171 Horseshoe Way
Richmond, BC
Canada V7A 4V4

First published in 2012

ISBN 10: 1-77132-035-4
ISBN 13: 978-1-77132-035-1

CEO and Publisher: Ben Lotfi
Author: Angela Adair
Editorial: Tricia Pope
Creative Director: Garett Chan
Art Director: Christine Covert
Design & Layout: Charmaine Muzyka
Production: James Badger, Mell D'Clute
Sourcing: Janny Lam
Photography: Devin Karringten

For more SpiceBox products and information, visit our website:
www.spicebox.ca

Manufactured in China

1 3 5 7 9 10 8 6 4 2

Contents

History

Beading could very well be the oldest art form known to humankind. Its history remains uncertain however, as the most archaic artifacts were strung on natural, degradable materials. Tangible evidence of ancient strung and woven necklaces are found primarily in burial grounds. The undisturbed, preserved bodies allow for the arrangement of stones and longer lasting materials like bones and shells to remain intact. We are blessed to bear witness to some traditional techniques and ceremonies involving beads in today's indigenous cultures, such as those in Africa, South East Asia, and North America, which reflect the customs of previous generations.

It is from her study of African bead weaving in the early 80s that artist and teacher Virginia Blakelock is attributed with recognizing the subtle yet integral difference of the "Right Angle Weave" from other beading styles. Unlike most other beading weaves, stitches and nettings, which are constructed in layers, Blakelock recognized a more geometric method of building structure in certain indigenous works, and thus a whole new avenue of structure. The Right Angle Weave in its current form might be considered a modern technique, though its concept can be found universally throughout traditional Europe, Russia, Africa and more.

Current

I first learned to weave with beads using the "one needle" technique, in which you work from one end of your thread to the next, passing through each bead several times to achieve proper tension and durability. This technique limited the material to very fine beading thread, which has a fabulous soft feel, but restricts structural possibilities because of the limpness of the final project. I went on to learn the many different beading weaves like the Bead Loom, the Peyote Stitch, and the Brick Stitch. When after 20 years of beading I was introduced to the Right Angle Weave, a light bulb went on over my head and I became excited by the possibilities.

I eventually came across new books with impossible looking graphs written in Japanese, and I became determined to learn to read them. I asked one of my Japanese students to bring a book back from Japan for me, and she presented me with the most hilarious pattern book for little crystal animals. Working with these patterns, I strove to master the concept of 3D structure in beads. There is no extra passing through the beads while creating these structures, which allows for experimentation with stronger stringing materials like elastic, steel stringing wire and half-hard wire. Then came the combinations of different beads, sizes, and colors. The possibilities in beading never end, and that's why I love it.

Tools

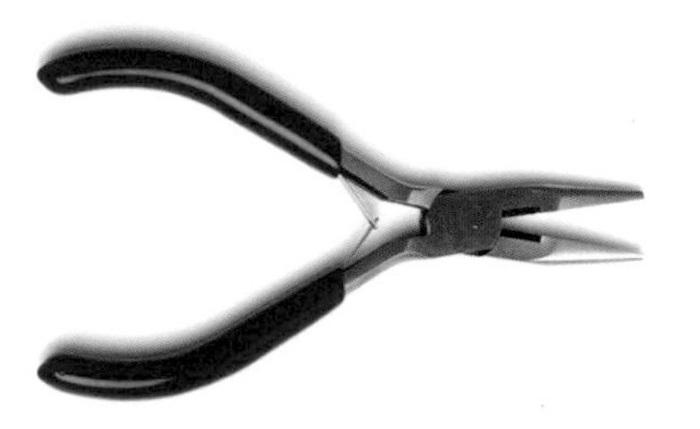

These basic beading tools are all you need for most beading techniques. Most of the projects in this book were written to be done without the need for special beading tools! Keep a pair of sharp scissors handy for cutting string, and a lighter for melting the ends.

Chain Nose Pliers

Chain nose pliers have a short, tapered, flat nose. They are your basic tool for opening and closing links, making bends in wire, and for crimping round-shaped crimping beads. Make sure your chain nose pliers are smooth on the inside of the nose.

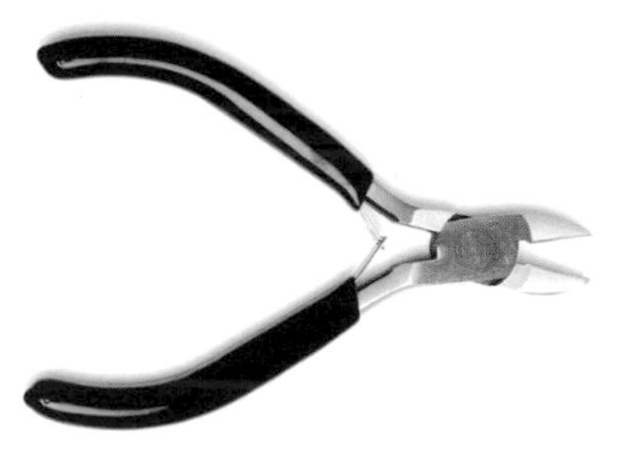

Angled Cutters

The edge of this tool is angled to fit closer to your work when you are cutting. Be sure to hold the flat side of the cutter closest to where you'd like to cut.

Round Nose Pliers

These pliers have a cone-shaped nose that allows you make round shapes in wire. This tool should not be used to open and close jump rings or for crimping. Choose round nose pliers that have a good variety of size in the cone shape.

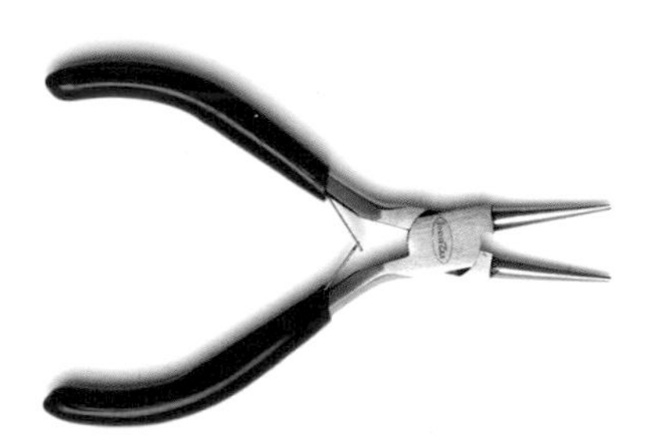

Crimping Tool

This is a special tool designed specifically for tube-shaped crimping beads. By using the two different indents in the nose, you first fold the crimping bead in half, and then again into a smooth, streamlined tube shape.

Beading Needles

These needles are essential if you are using beading thread and seed beads together. Use a smaller needle if your technique requires you to pass through the beads several times. The size is described by a number, usually between 10 and 15; the higher the number, the smaller the gauge of the needle.

Beading Tray

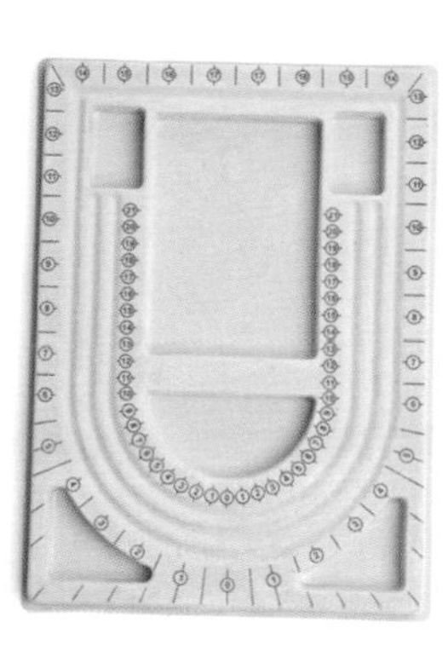

These trays are used to prevent your beads from rolling around, and to help you imagine the shape and design of your project. They are usually marked with inches and centimeters for reference when sizing your work.

Beading Glue

This is usually a form of rubber cement. There are many types of glue so be sure yours dries clear and will adhere to the materials you are using. This is usually listed on the label. The surface you are gluing should always be dry and clean.

Findings

There are thousands of metal components in the world of beading meant to help you design your work the way you like. The following are some of the most commonly used in making jewelry.

Calotte (Clamshell)

A calotte, or clamshell, is designed to anchor around a knot, bead, or crimping bead. It has an open clamshell shape, with a loop on it for attaching to a clasp or other finding. Some calottes open from the top, and others from the side.

Crimping Beads

These are small beads made of soft metal, meant to clamp onto stringing wire to attach clasps and secure beads in place. Round crimping beads are used with chain nose pliers, and tube-shaped crimping beads are used with a crimping tool.

Clasps

A clasp is attached to jewelry so you can open and close it to take it on and off. Choose a clasp that you find easy to use, and that stays secure while wearing it.

Jump Rings

These little rings are made from half-hard wire and are used to attach the links of findings to each other. Jump rings should always be opened from front to back, not pulled into a U-shape.

Headpins & Eyepins

Headpins are short pieces of half-hard wire, hammered on the bottom to hold a bead or beads. The wire is formed into a loop at the top to attach to an ear wire, or to otherwise attach to another finding as a dangle. Eyepins are similar to headpins, except that one end is turned into a loop, which can be attached to the loop of a headpin to make a longer earring or dangle.

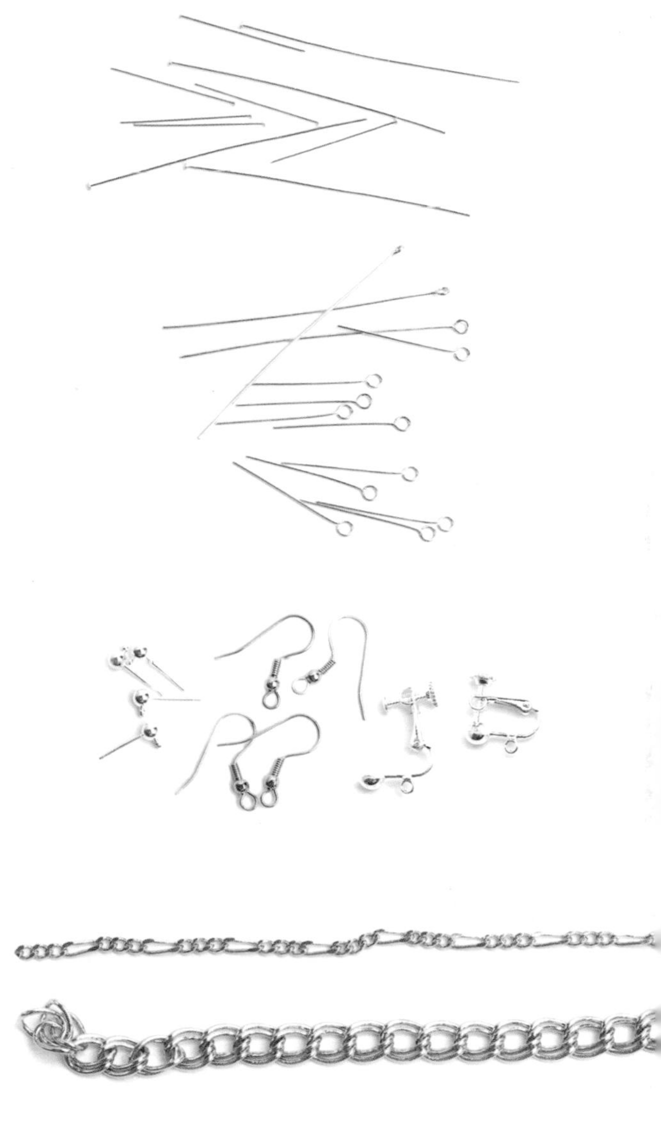

Ear Wires

These are attached to an earring so you can wear them, and should have a loop that can be opened for attaching beadwork.

Chain

Chain is usually sold by the length and can be cut with cutting pliers to suit your design. Chain comes in links of many sizes, and is used with jump rings to attach to a clasp.

Cell Phone Charm

This finding is somewhat less common, but is the perfect device for attaching beaded decorations to your electronic devices.

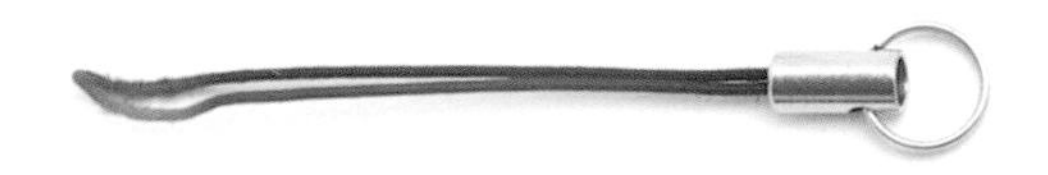

String & Wire

This page shows the most modern products for stringing and working with beads. Choose the stringing material according to your project and the size and shape of your beads.

Stringing Wire

This string is made of tiny steel wires, twisted together into a fine cable, and coated in nylon. It comes in a variety of diameters and number of strands; fewer strands usually means the wire is stiffer.

Half-hard Wire

This metal wire is used for making beaded chain and metal links as it holds its shape when you bend and curl it. It comes in many kinds of metals, finishes, and diameters.

Nylon Beading Thread

Cotton or polyester sewing thread is very seldom strong enough for beading and will usually break as you are working with it. Nylon thread for weaves and stitches is sold in beading stores. It is much stronger, and often waxed to make it easier to work with. This thread is the best choice for techniques that require you to double several times through your beads.

Silk Thread

Silk thread is very delicate, and should generally be knotted between strung beads or used when sewing beads onto silk fabric. It is not as resistant to moisture as nylon thread, but has a much softer feel and drape. Silk thread is usually sold on cards with the needle already attached for a streamlined pass through the tiny holes of pearls.

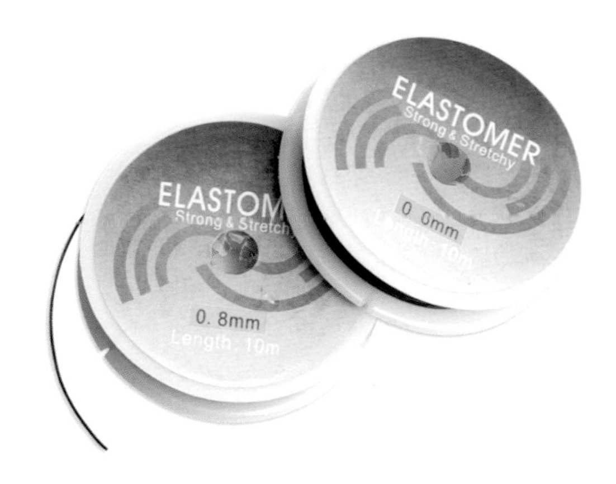

Elastic Cord

There are many new elastic products that are very stretchy and strong, and are great for beading. Some are stiff enough to use without a needle and will not fray. Be sure to choose the right size for your beads, and consider how many times you need to pass through them.

Fishing Line

Some beading projects can be done with everyday fishing line. Be sure it is strong yet flexible, and measures 0.3mm - 0.4mm in diameter. While special beading line is best for strength and flexibility, the main advantage of fishing line is its transparency, which looks best with crystal clear beads. All of the projects in this book can be made with fishing line.

Beads

Seed Beads

These are the smallest beads, and the most commonly found because of their low price and versatility. They are found in a wide range of colors and qualities, and like beading needles, their number rating increases as the beads get smaller. Some seed beads may cost a little more, but have a more uniform shape and longer lasting finish.

Crystals

Crystal beads are made of glass containing extra lead, which causes more light to refract from the surface. Very sparkly and flashy, crystal beads are usually cut like gemstones.

Stones

Stones have been used for many centuries for their color and symbolism. Mined from the earth, they are priced according to their rarity and purity. Some stones are artificially enhanced to improve the look and color, and all can be faceted, shaped, and polished.

Lamp Working Beads

These beads are handmade by melting torch-heated glass over a turning mandrel. Cooling the glass layer by layer allows for capturing images in the glass, and creating endless shape and color combinations.

Fire Polish Glass

These glass beads are uniformly faceted and fired in a special way, which leaves a durable glaze on the surface and a shiny finish.

Pearls

A century ago, pearls were worth more than diamonds, and the most perfectly round and creamy colored pearls were valued by royalty all over the world. The invention of freshwater pearls led to broader affordability and to this day, pearls are cultured in many shapes and colored in different ways. Glass pearls are generally more affordable, and shaped perfectly round. In Baroque times they were made of blown glass. Today the round shape is formed around a plastic mandrel.

Silver & Gold

Precious metal beads are more costly, but will last much longer and can be re-polished. Sterling silver must usually be stamped with 92.5, which stands for the percentage of silver to other alloys. Gold fill beads and findings are much less expensive than solid gold and unlike plated metals, the gold will not rub off.

Plated Metal

Plated metal beads are less expensive, but the metallic plating is not always durable and the beads cannot be re-polished.

Pewter

Pewter beads look like antiqued silver, but are made of several different metals and cost much less.

How to Use this Book

Bead weaving involves one or more strings sharing the hole of different beads in different sorts of formations. The repetition of these formations will determine the look, feel, and flexibility of the final project. As its name suggests, the **Right Angle Weave** is geometrically constructed; the number of beads you use in each stitch, as well as the shape and size of the beads, will determine the outcome.

Asymmetrical shape; some curve and bevel to make 3D shapes and figures.

Doubling Through Beads

There are only two ways to enter a bead: from one side or the other. Entering the bead from opposite directions will brace the shape round. This allows for a geometric shape. Unless otherwise mentioned, assume you will be doubling though beads in this way when instructed to.

Entering the bead from the same direction can distort the shape and make it asymmetrical.

As this way of sharing the bead is not as common in the Right Angle Weave, it will be noted in the instructions when it is necessary—most often when attaching to a calotte or creating flowers.

Connecting Beads

By reading through the diagrams, you can see that each project is created from a series of little round groups of beads. These separate groups are like panels, and will be referred to as such in the instructions. The number of beads used in each panel will determine the angle of the weave and the shape in 3D projects. The numbers provided in each pattern are approximate. You may need to use more (or fewer) beads on occasion. The size of the beads used will vary the texture and shape of the finished work.

What do we mean by "Upper", "Lower", etc.?

As the weaving becomes more complex, the instructions will sometimes refer to certain strings as being upper, lower, inside or outside. It will not be helpful to label the strings as one or the other; the two strings are always trading positions. These written instructions are to help you know which string is doing which action, and will make sense visually as you compare your work to the diagrams.

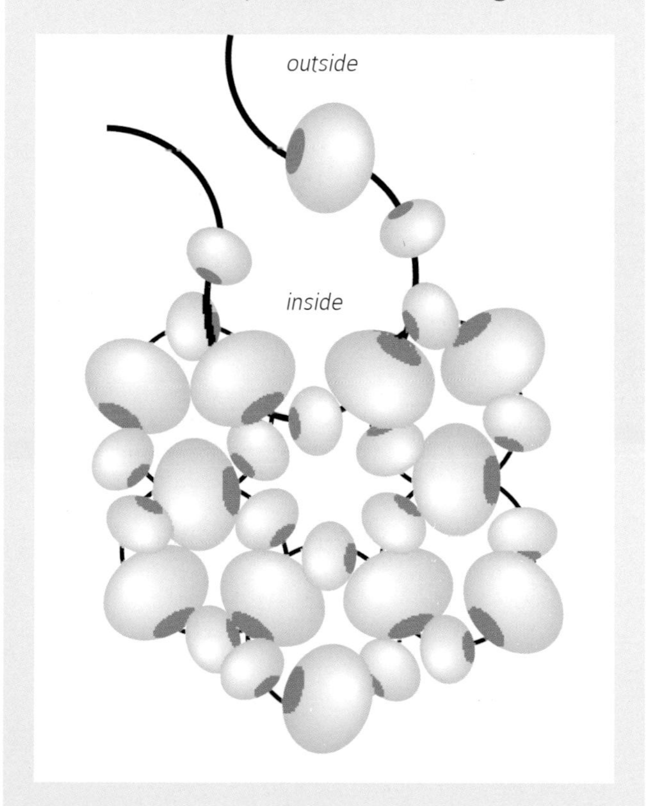

Simple Rings

These easy projects use a simple, symmetrical weave and will warm you up for more complicated patterns. Using smaller beads with a smooth finish will result in a comfortable ring. Uniformly shaped beads will keep the shape more even, though experimenting with different beads is half the fun! If you are completely new to beading, I recommend practicing a ring or two before moving on to the more challenging projects in the book. Remember to keep your tension tight as you work; this means pulling both strings when instructed to.

Materials

- 18 in/45 cm of string
- 12 size-6 seed beads
- 60 size-10 seed beads

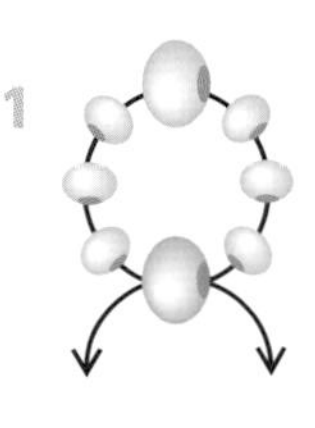

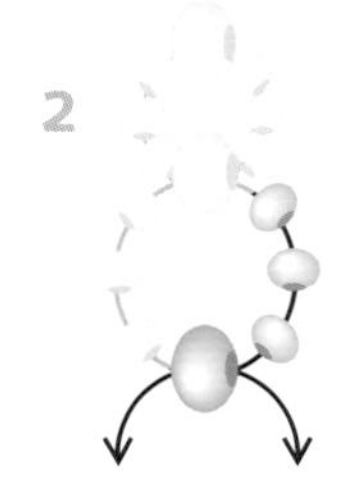

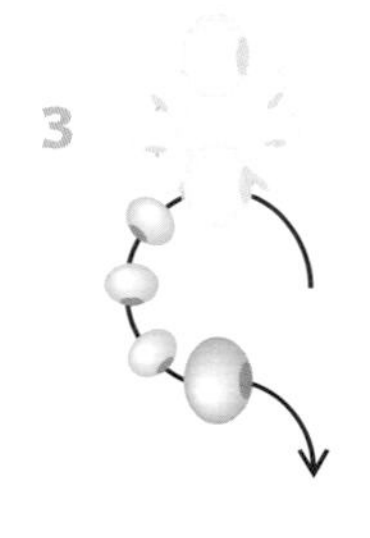

Instructions

1. Place eight seed beads on the string. Alternate one size-6 seed bead with three size-10 seed beads. Pull the beads to the very center of the string, and double back around and through the first size-6 seed bead. When you pull the strings tight, leave both ends the same length. They will create one panel, and the strings should be in position to make another panel attached to the first one.

2. Place four seed beads on one string. Alternate three size-10 seed beads with one size-6 seed bead.

3. On the other string, place three size-10 seed beads. Double both strings through the last size-6 seed bead. Pull both strings tight.

4. Repeat the steps to create another panel connected to the last. Repeat the steps to create another twelve panels or enough panels to fit around your finger.

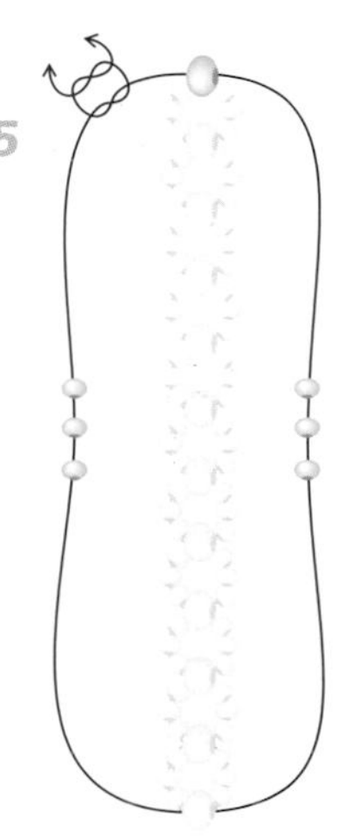

5. On each string, place three size-10 seed beads. Pass one string through the very first size-6 seed bead. Be sure to enter the bead from the same side as the string you are currently passing, or the ring will be twisted.

6 & 7. Make a knot with the two strings and pull very tight. Then, make the second and pull tight. You may find it easier to make the knot tight if you grip the string using chain nose pliers. Cut the string ends to about 2 mm in length, using small scissors or nail clippers. Use a lighter to melt the ends into the knot, which will smooth out and seal the knot. Hold the lighter with one hand, and carefully move the string ends closer to the blue part of the flame, pulling back quickly as soon as it melts. The plastic will cool quickly. Take your finger and push the melted end into the knot.

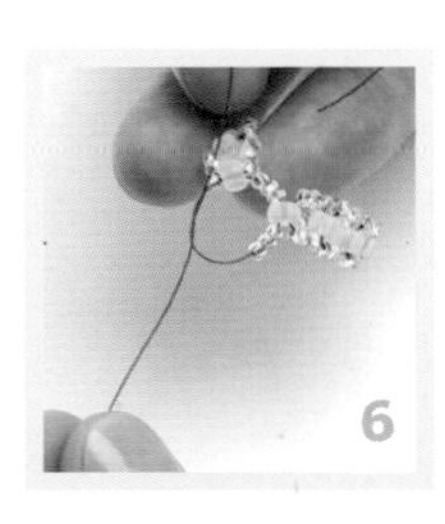

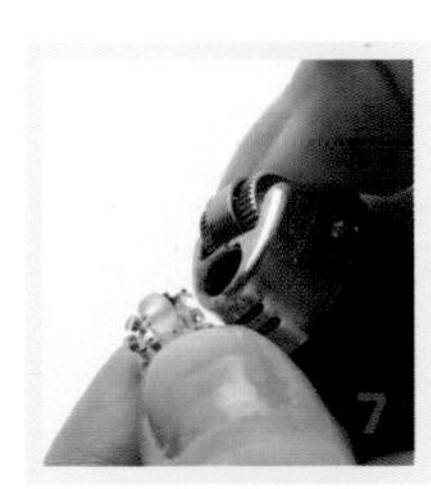

Ring Variation

Materials

- 18 in/45 cm of string
- 10 size-6 seed beads
- 52 size-10 seed beads

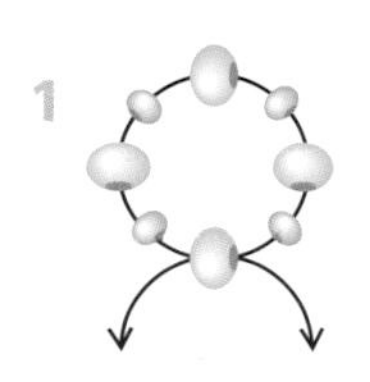

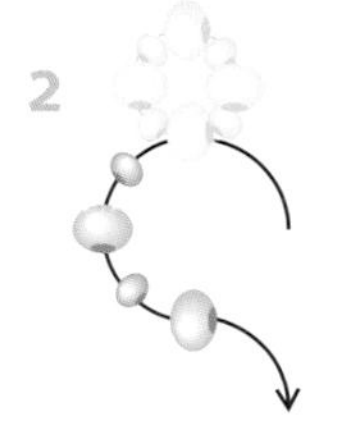

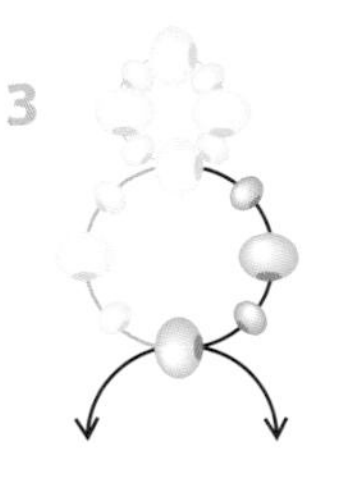

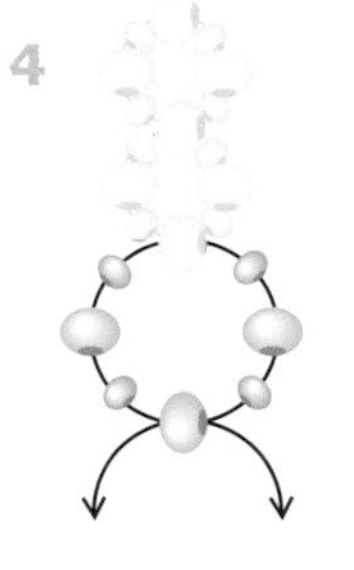

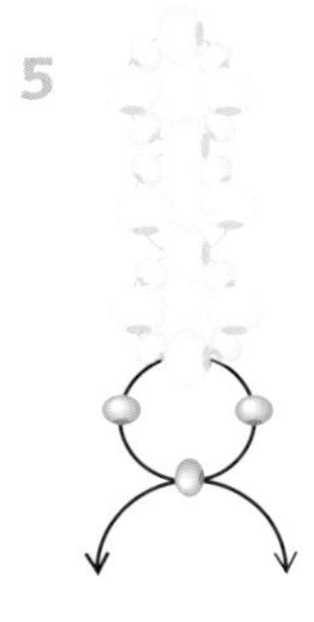

Instructions

1. Place eight seed beads on the string. Alternate one size-6 seed bead with one size-10 seed bead. Pull the beads to the very center of the string, and double back around and through the first size-6 seed bead.

2. When you pull the strings tight, leave both ends the same length. They will create one panel, and the strings should be in position to make another panel attached to the first one. Place four seed beads on one string. Alternate one size-10 seed bead with one size-6 seed bead.

3. On the other string, place one size-10 seed bead, one size-6 seed bead, and one size-10 seed bead.

4. Double both strings through the last size-10 seed bead. Pull both strings tight. Repeat these steps to create another panel connected to the last.

5. On one string place two size-10 seed beads. On the other string, place one size-10 seed bead. Double both strings through the second size-10 seed bead.

6. Pull both strings tight. Repeat the previous steps ten times, or until the strip fits around your finger, pulling the string tight with each panel you make.

7. On each string, place one size-10 seed bead. Pass one string through the very first size-6 seed bead. Be sure to enter the bead from the same side as the string you are currently passing, or the ring will be twisted. Using two very tight knots, finish the string ends (see step 7 on page 17).

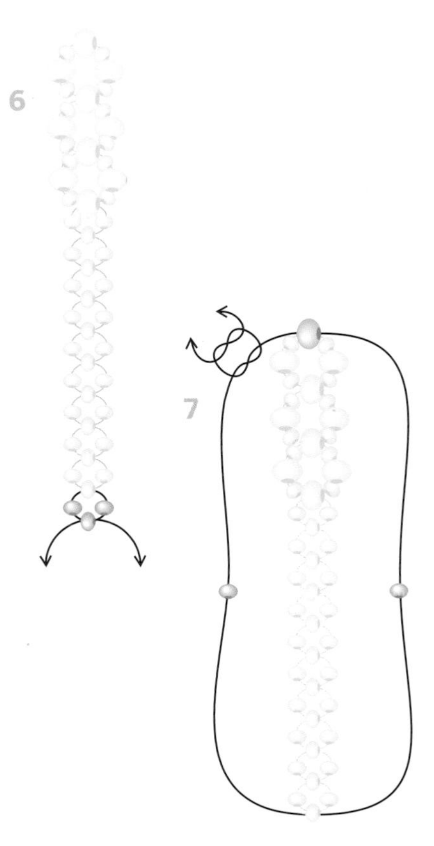

Crystal Bracelet

You can use seed beads to make this bracelet, but building it using crystals adds just enough sparkle to make it the perfect accessory for a night out. This bracelet as shown uses eight **"beaded beads"**. You may need to use more (or less) to make the bracelet fit you. For this project, you will need to use round nose pliers.

Materials to make 1 Beaded Bead

- 1 ft/30 cm of string
- 12 size-6 seed beads

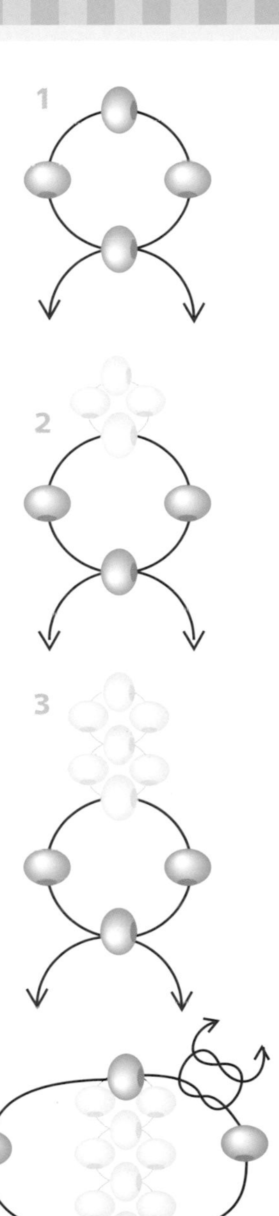

Instructions

How to make the beaded bead

1. Place four size-6 seed beads on the string. Pull the beads to the very center of the string.

Double around and through the first size-6 seed bead.

Pull both ends tight.

2. Place two size-6 seed beads on one end of string. On the other end of string, place one size-6 seed bead. Double through the second size-6 seed bead.

Pull both strings tight.

3. Place two size-6 seed beads on one end of string. On the other end of string, place one size-6 seed bead.

Double through the second size-6 seed bead. Pull both strings tight.

Repeat these steps to create three panels that are connected in a line.

4. On each string, place one size-6 seed bead. Pass one string through the very first size-6 seed bead. Be sure to enter this bead from the same side as the string you are currently passing. Using two very tight knots, finish the string ends (see step 7 on page 17).

Materials

- 1 ft/30 cm of string for every "beaded bead"
- 14 3-6 mm crystals for every "beaded bead"
- 2 8 mm crystals
- 2 ft/60 cm 20 g silver plated copper (or other) half-hard wire
- Toggle clasp to match wire

Instructions

How to make the Crystal Bracelet

1. On the 20 g wire, place one 4 mm crystal, one beaded bead and one 4 mm crystal. Using chain nose pliers, make a bend 1 cm in length at a 90 degree angle at the one end of the wire.

2. Choosing the appropriate size on the nose of the round nose pliers, shape the short piece of wire into a round loop. Start rolling your round nose pliers from the very tip of the wire.

3. Keep your pliers perpendicular to the wire in order to keep the loop straight up and down. Make sure your loop is closed, and ideally as round as possible. Pull the beads tight against the first loop.

4. Grab the wire tight against the beads using the very smallest point of the chain nose pliers. Fold the wire over the pliers at a 90 degree angle. Cut the wire end with angled cutters, leaving a 1 cm bend.

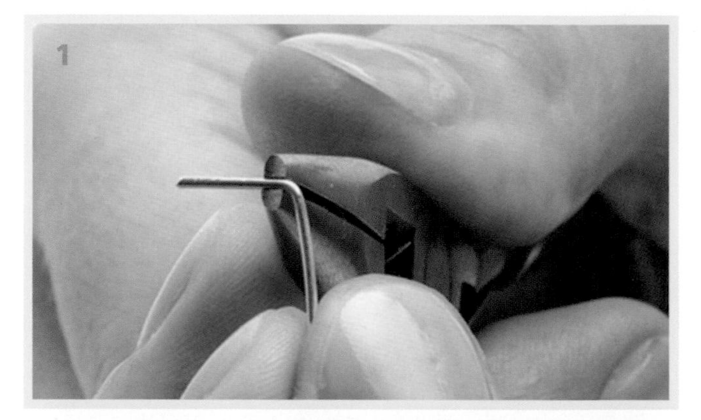
1

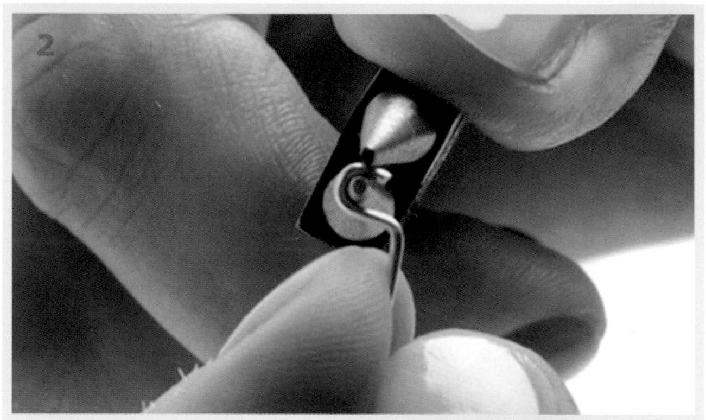
2

4

5. Use your round nose pliers to turn the end of wire into a round, closed loop. Repeat these steps for each beaded bead link, or switch the beaded bead for an 8 mm crystal when desired.

6. When attaching the links together, use the chain nose pliers to pull the loop open towards yourself, not into a U-shape.

7. Place the link you are attaching onto the ring and close the loop in the same way, keeping the shape round. Be sure the loop is completely closed. Attach the two parts of the toggle clasp to each end in the same way.

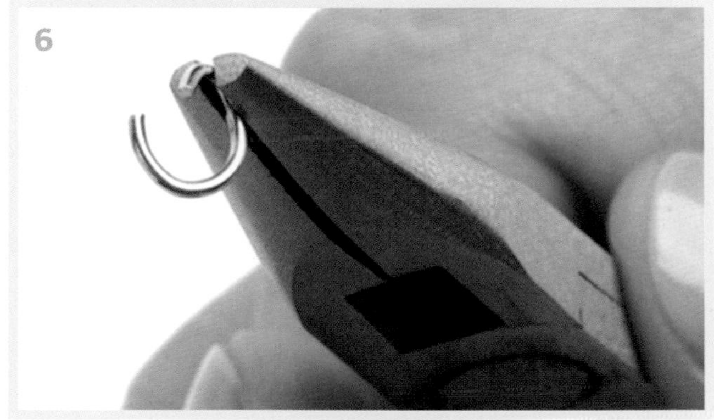

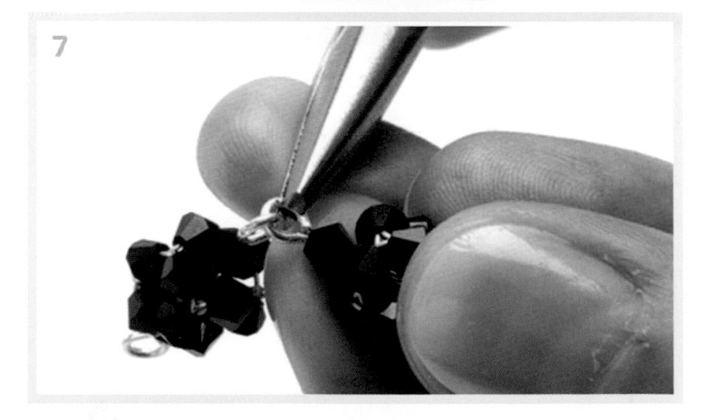

Victorian Lace Bracelet

This pattern imitates lace and the elaborate whimsy of Victorian times. The weave is flat, involving a combination of panels using different sizes and numbers of beads. Make your own divine bracelet using delicate colors and beads of your choice.

Materials

- 3 ft/1 m of string
- 44 4 mm glass beads - color A
- 11 4 mm glass beads - color B
- 152 size-10 seed beads
- 2 calottes
- 2 jump rings
- 1 lobster claw

Instructions

1. Place one size-10 seed bead on the string and pull to the center. Pass both strings down through the opening of the calotte. Pull both ends of the string to the same length and close the calotte around the size-10 seed bead.

2 & 3. Pass both ends through another size-10 seed bead, entering from the same side. On one string, place two size-10 seed beads.

4, 5 & 6. On the other string, place one size-10 seed bead. Double through the last size-10 seed bead. Pull both strings tight. On each string place two size-10 seed beads. Double through the second size-10 seed bead. Pull both ends tight. On one string place a 4 mm glass bead.

7, 8 & 9. On the same string place five size-10 seed beads. Double around and through the first size-10 seed bead. Pull the doubled seed bead loop and the 4 mm glass bead tight against the last group of beads. Repeat these steps on the other string.

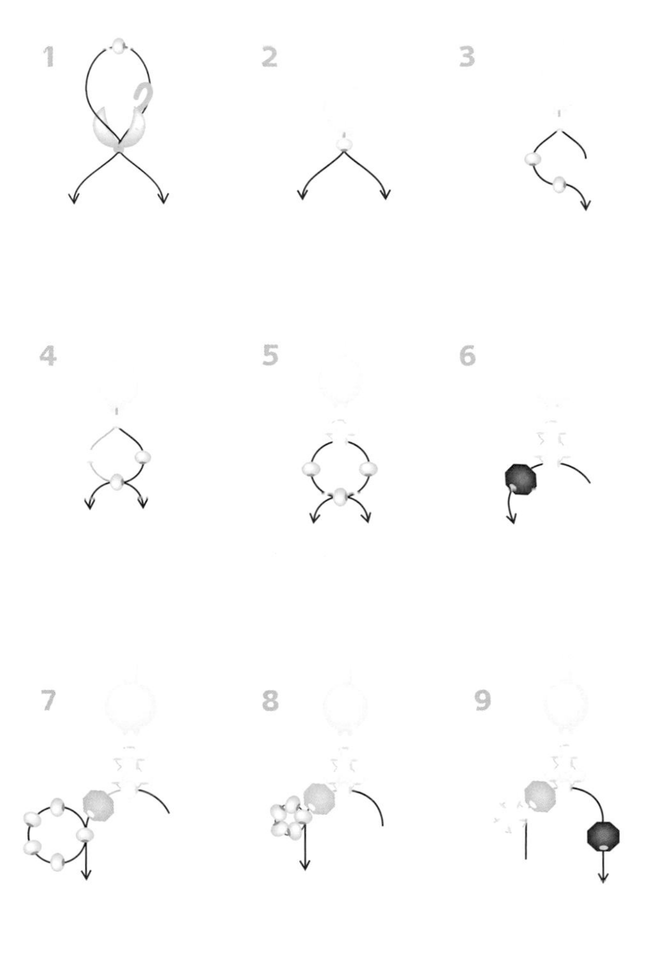

NOTE: *When measuring your length, don't forget to account for the length of your clasp. The project shown uses eleven repetitions of the pattern, and comfortably fits a 6 inch wrist.*

10 & 11. Double both strings through a 4 mm glass bead. Pass each string through the next size-10 seed bead of the previous panel of five. You may need to bend the work to get at the bead's opening. The work is quite tight in this pattern.

12. **a)** On one string, place a 4 mm glass bead on the other string place one size-10 bead. Double both strings through one size-10 seed bead. Pull both strings tight. **b)** On one string place two size-10 seed beads and on the other, place one. Double through the second size-10 seed bead. Repeat steps to continue weaving the bracelet until it is long enough to fit your wrist.

13. **a)** On each string, place one size-10 seed bead. Pass both strings through another size-10 bead, entering from the same side. Pull both strings tight. **b)** Pass both strings up through the second calotte. On one string, place a size-10 seed bead. **c)** Using two very tight knots, finish the string ends. Using chain nose pliers, close the calotte.

14. **ATTACHING THE CLASP:** Use round nose pliers to round out and close the loops on each calotte. Using chain nose pliers, open the jump ring by locating the opening and pulling the open end forward. Remember, do not open it into a U-shape. Holding the open jump ring with pliers, slip in the loop of the calotte and the clasp. Close the jump ring by pushing the open end back until the ring is closed, with no space between the two ends. On the other end, attach a single jump ring to the other calotte. The lobster claw will fasten to it.

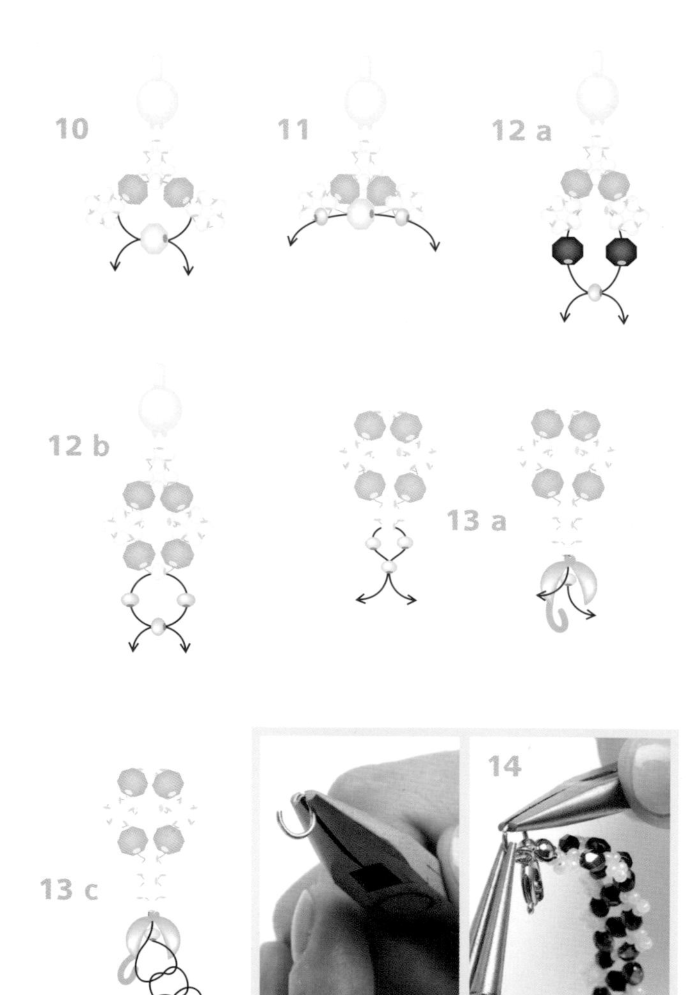

This bracelet was made using the Victorian Lace bracelet pattern and shows just what a big difference different types of beads make in the finished product.

Cocktail Ring

Materials

- 2 ft/60 cm of string
- 18 4 mm glass beads
- 48 size-10 seed beads

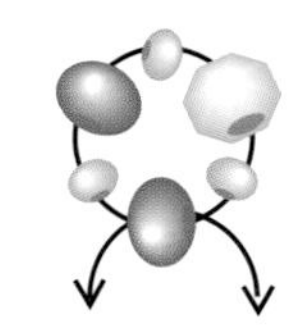

Nothing shows your fun side like an oversized ring! After a little practice, this ring will be a snap to make and you will easily develop your own color ideas.

This project moves away from connecting multiples of four, and introduces working in multiples of three, which creates a more hexagonal arrangement. I have provided a few of my favorite combinations using this pattern. You'll have fun coming up with your own!

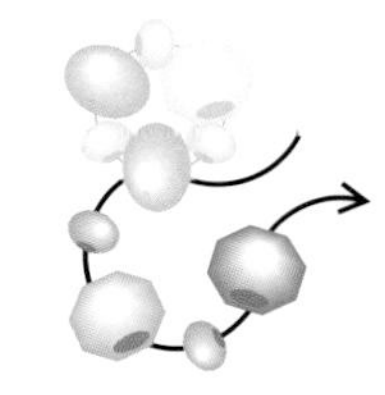

Instructions

1. Place six seed beads on the string. Alternate one size-6 seed bead or 4 mm glass bead with one size-10 seed bead. Pull beads to the center of the string. Double through the first size-6 seed bead. Pull both strings tight, leaving two equal lengths of string.

2. Place four seed beads on one string. Alternate one size-10 seed bead with one size-6 seed bead or 4 mm glass bead.

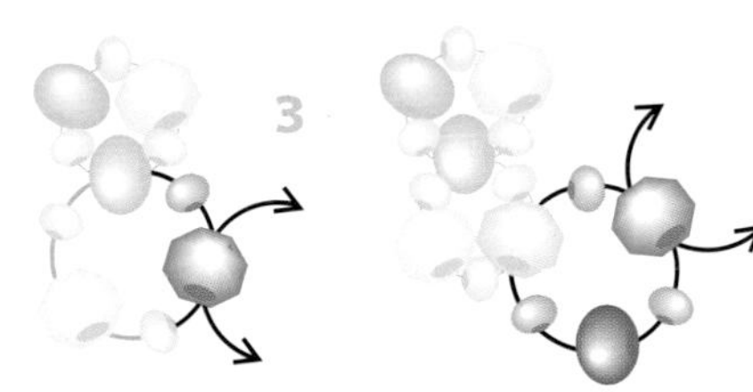

3. On the other string, place one size-10 seed bead. Double both strings through the last size-6 seed bead or 4 mm glass bead. Pull both strings tight. From this point on you must be sure to add the larger quantity of beads to the outside of the curve. This will ensure that the shape continues curving and ends up as a flat circular panel.

4. Place four seed beads on the outside string. Alternate one size-10 seed bead and one size-6 seed bead or 4 mm glass bead. On the inside string, place one size-10 seed bead. Double both strings through the last size-6 seed bead or 4 mm glass bead. Pull both strings tight. Follow these steps until you have created five connected panels in total.

5. On the inside string, place one size-10 seed bead. Pass through the very first size-6 seed bead or 4 mm glass bead.

6. On each string, place a size-10 seed bead. Double both strings through one size-6 seed bead or 4 mm glass bead.

7. On one string place one size-10 seed bead. Pass through the next size-6 seed bead or 4 mm glass bead.

8. Continue adding a size-10 seed bead and passing through the next size-6 seed bead or 4 mm glass bead until you have added six in total. You will have passed through the same bead the other string is exiting. Pull both strings tight.

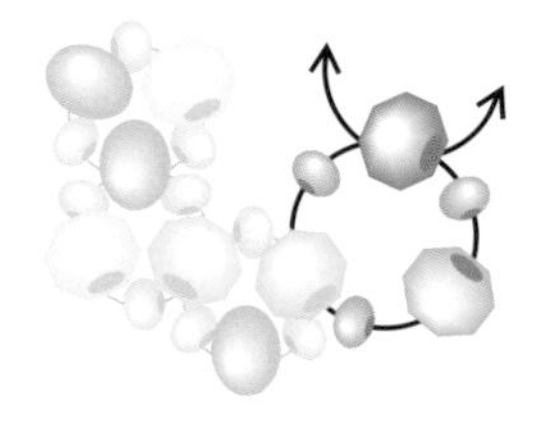

4

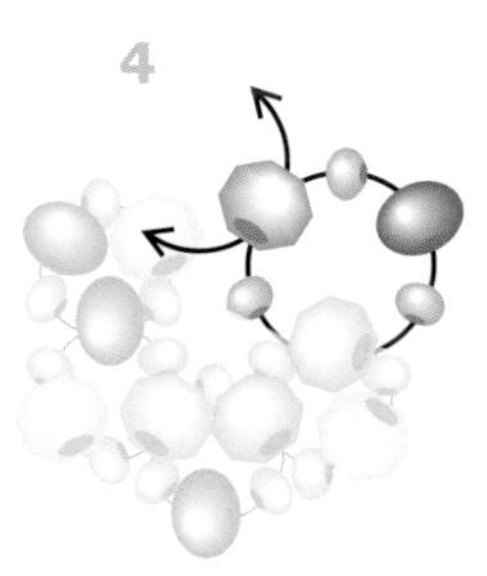

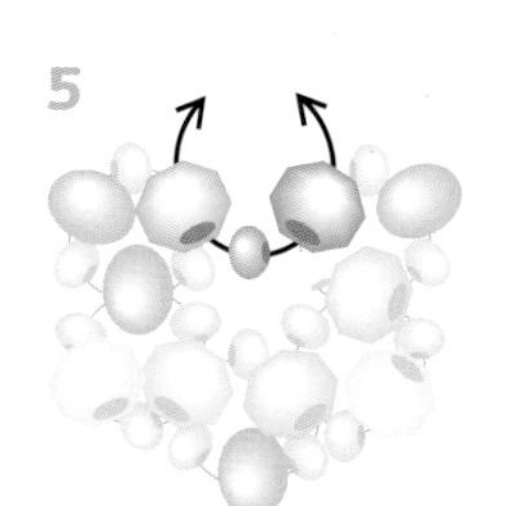

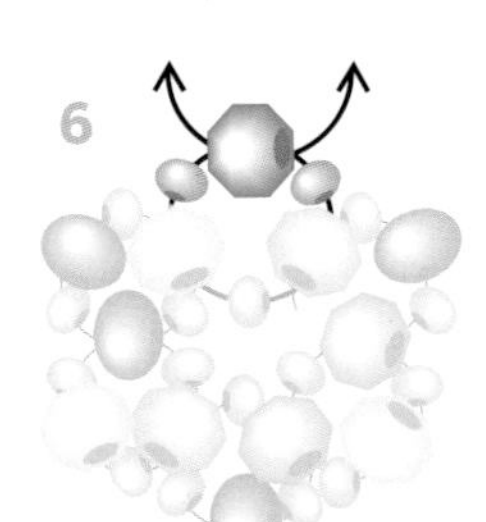

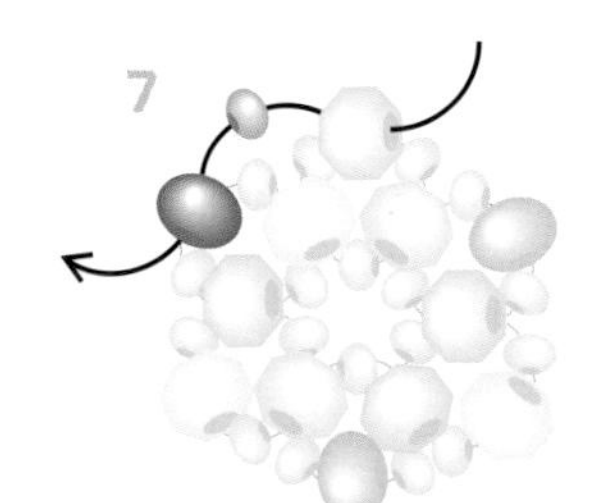

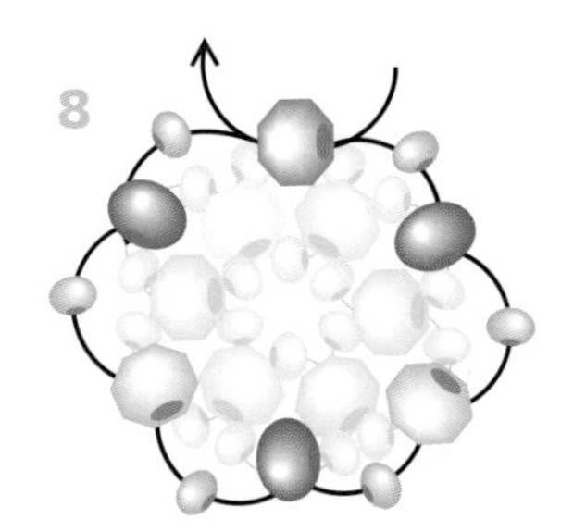

9. Double both strings through a size-10 seed bead, entering from opposite sides of the bead. On each string place one size-10 seed bead. Double through a size-10 seed bead. Pull both strings tight.

10. On each string place three size-10 seed beads. Repeat these steps until you reach your desired size for the ring. On each string place three size-10 seed beads. Pass one string through the very opposite size-6 seed bead or 4 mm glass bead. Be sure to enter the bead from the same side as the end of string you are currently passing, or the ring will be twisted. Using two very tight knots, finish the string ends.

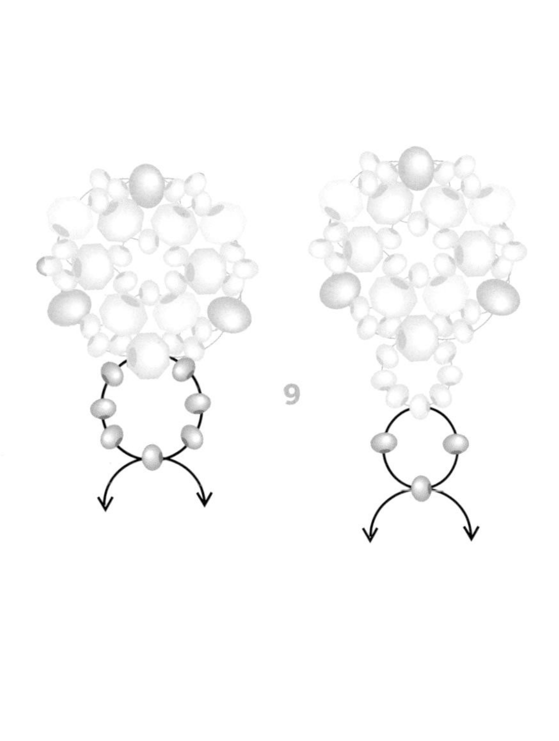

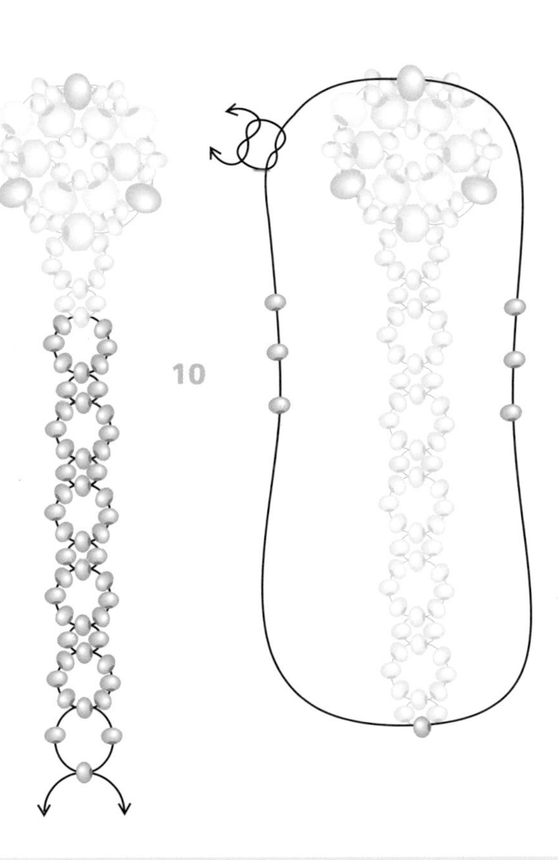

Costume Bracelet

Materials

- 2 ft / 60 cm of string
- 18 4 mm glass beads
- 48 size-10 seed beads

TIP: Remember to keep your tension tight by pulling both the strings after every step.

TIP: If your settings are different colors, decide the order in which they will sit in the bracelet.

A bangle slips on any wrist. In this pattern links can be added or removed for a better fit. The hexagonal charms are treated as though they were a setting, and the finer weaving connects them as in the links of a costume bracelet.

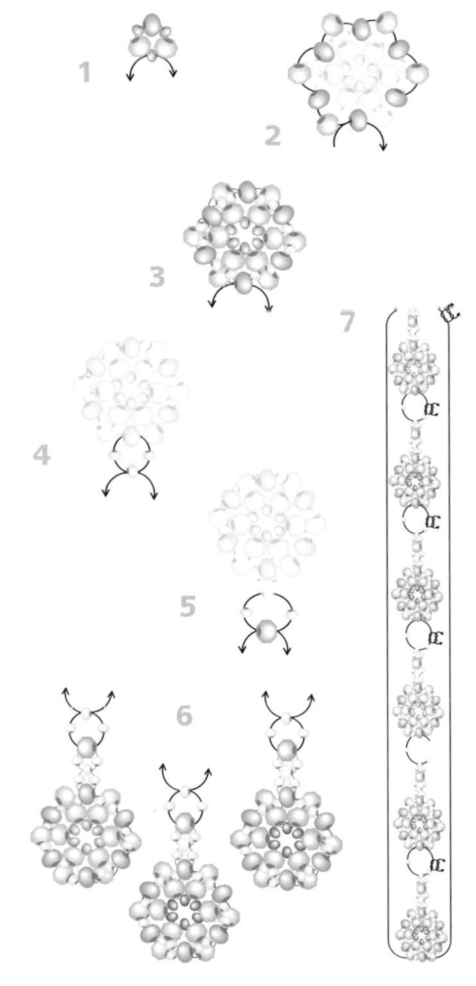

Instructions

1. **MAKING THE SETTING:** Cut 1 ft / 30 cm of string. Follow the cocktail ring pattern until step 8 on page 30 to make the individual settings. Make two settings of each color, or choose your own combination for six in total.

2 & 3. On one string place a 4 mm glass bead. Pass through the next 4 mm glass bead from the previous layer. Continue adding one 4 mm glass bead then passing through the next 4 mm glass bead from the previous layer, until you have added six beads in total.

4. On each string, place one size-10 seed bead. Double through one size-10 seed bead. Pull both strings tight.

5. On each string, place one size-10 seed bead. Double through one 4 mm glass bead. On each string, place one size-10 seed bead.

6. Double both strings through one size-10 seed bead. Pull both strings tight. After you have finished making all six of the settings for the bracelet, you will connect them.

7. On each string, place one size-10 seed bead. Pass one string through the size-6 seed bead in the next link. You will find that your settings are slightly curved; make sure they are all curved the in the same direction as you attach them so your bracelet is shaped nicely. Continue connecting the settings together in order, and finishing the ends until all six are connected. Using two very tight knots, finish the string ends (see step 7 on page 17).

Cartoon Kitten

Materials

- 3 ft/1 m of fishing line
- 50 size-8 seed beads for the body
- 11 size-10 seed beads, assorted colors for toes, nose, tips of ears and tail
- 2 4 mm glass or round faceted crystal beads for the eyes

Different 3D shapes can be made using the Right Angle Weave, and the shapes are determined by the number of beads in each little group you connect. What is key when working with 3D shapes is to make sure you pull the strings tight at the end of each step. This kitten pattern is a great introduction to creating forms. The head is a bigger, rounder shape than the smaller, squarish body.

My cartoon kittens are made from uniformly squarish seed beads. The result is a very smooth and evenly shaped cartoon cat. Experiment with different beads. You will be surprised at the whole new personality your little kitten can have with a bit of variation.

TIP: The star denotes the center of the piece.

Instructions:

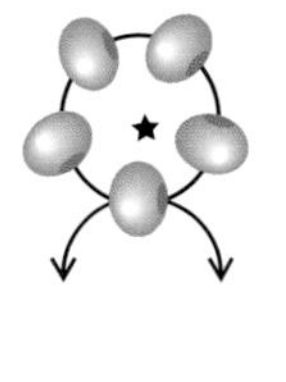

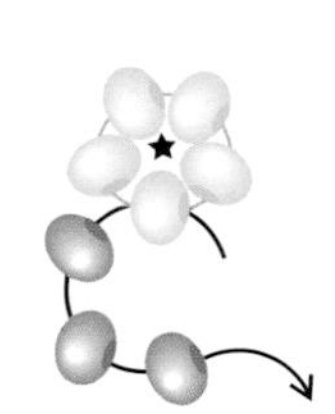

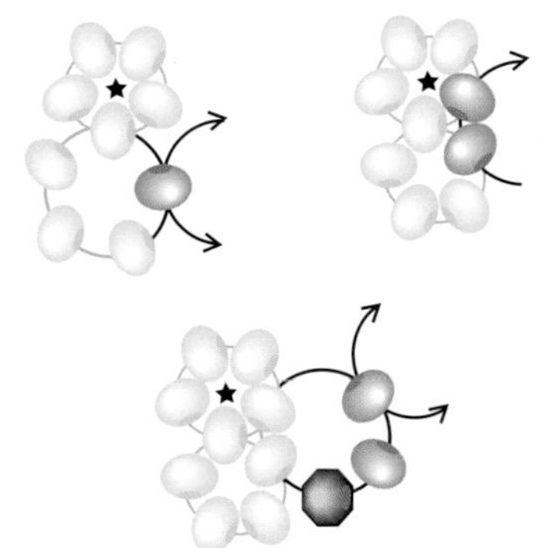

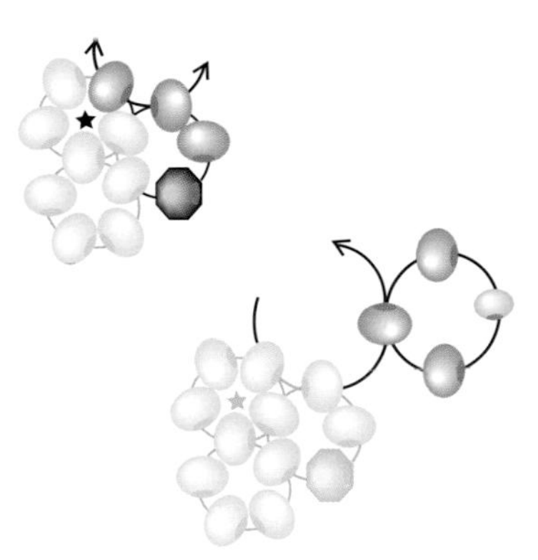

1 & 2. Place five size-8 seed beads on the string and pull them to the very center. Double both strings through the first bead. This panel of five beads is the first "layer" — the kitten's forehead. Place four size-8 seed beads on one string. Double through the last bead.

3. Pass the lower string through the next bead in the previous layer. Place one 4 mm glass bead (for the kitten's eye), and two size-8 seed beads on the upper string. Double through the last bead.

4. Pass the lower string through the next bead in the previous layer of five beads. On the upper string place two size-8 seed beads, one size-10 seed bead and one size-8 seed bead (for the kitten's first ear). Double around and through the first size-8 seed bead.

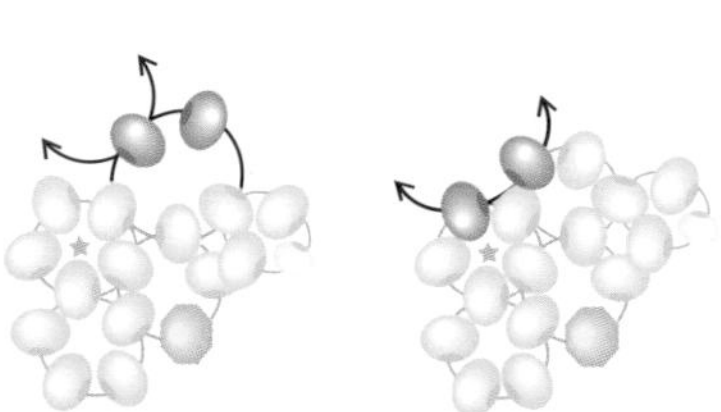

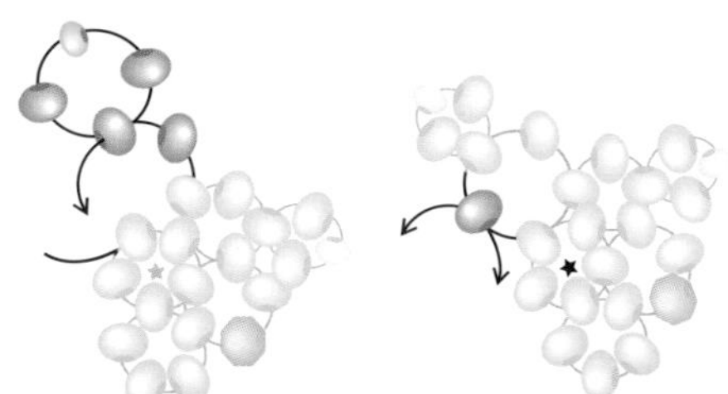

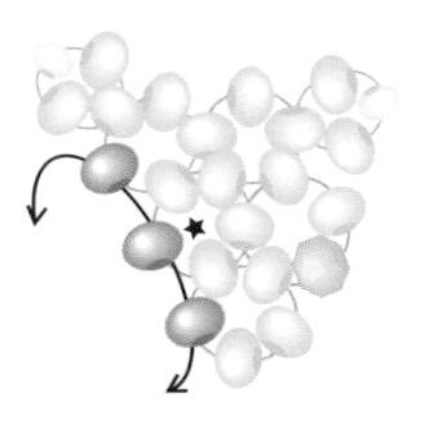

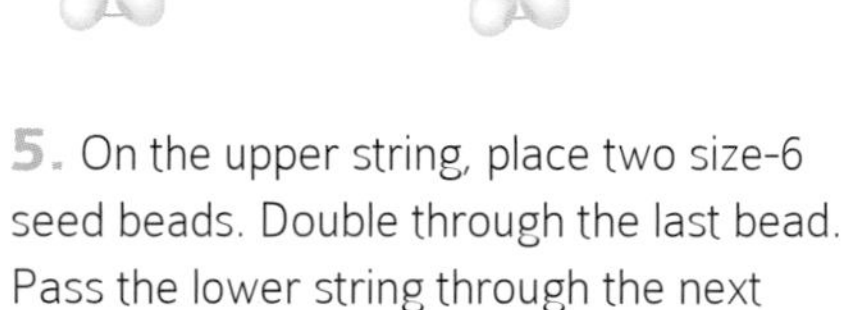

5. On the upper string, place two size-6 seed beads. Double through the last bead. Pass the lower string through the next bead in the previous layer of beads.

6. On the upper string place three size-8 seed beads, one size-10 seed bead, and one size-8 seed bead. Double around and through the second size-8 seed bead. On the upper string place one more size-8 seed bead. Double through this last bead.

7. Pass through the last bead of the previous layer, as well as the very first seed bead from the second layer.

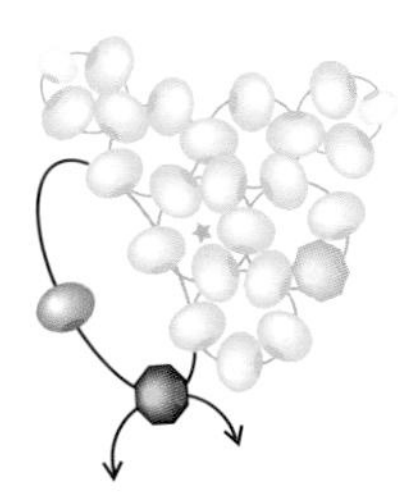

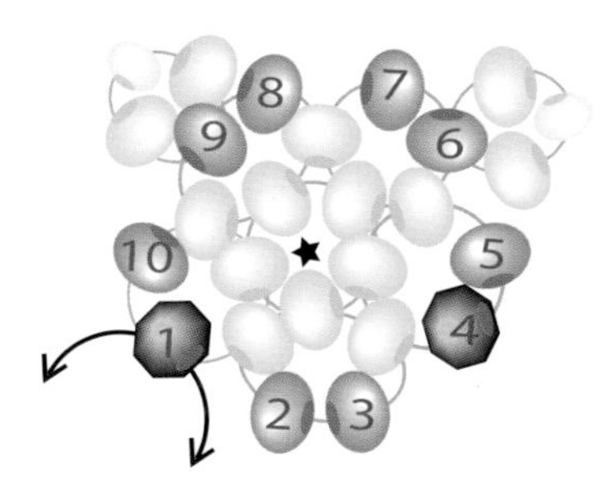

8. On the upper string, place one size-8 seed bead and one 4 mm glass bead for the kitten's other eye. Double through the 4 mm glass bead.

9. Pull both strings very tight. You should now have completed the first half of a very cute kitten head, with six connected panels in total. Make sure the ears are poking out the outside of the kitten's head. If your kitten is looking less than cute, it's a good idea to check the diagram and fix any mistakes here. When necessary, pull the work open with your fingers to remove the woven beads, and follow the instructions again. The middle of the kitten's head is a rim of ten beads in five groups of two.

TIP: In the following diagrams, some beads are removed to make steps clearer.

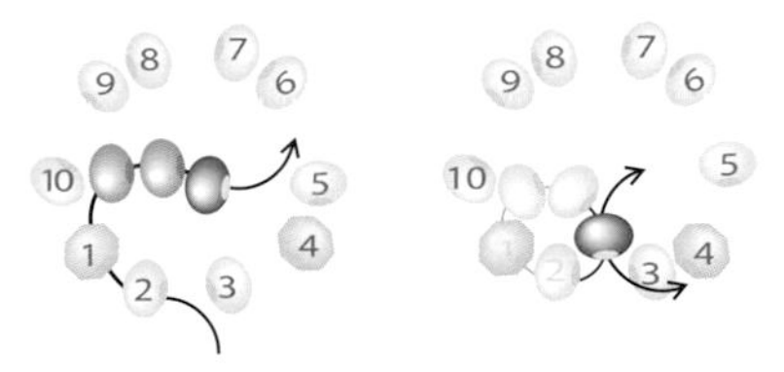

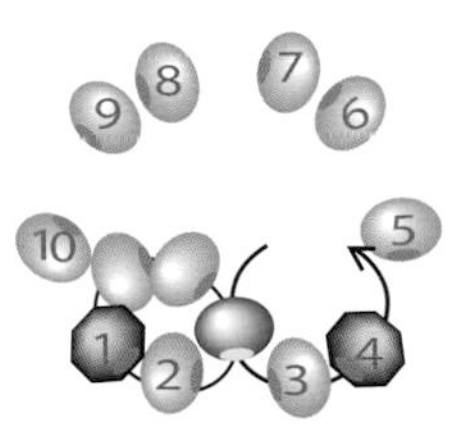

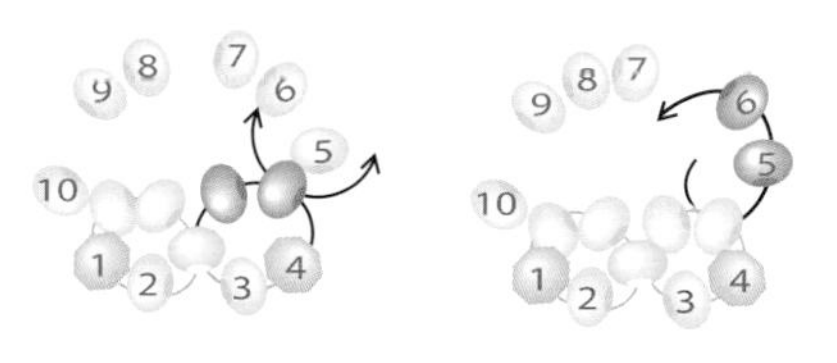

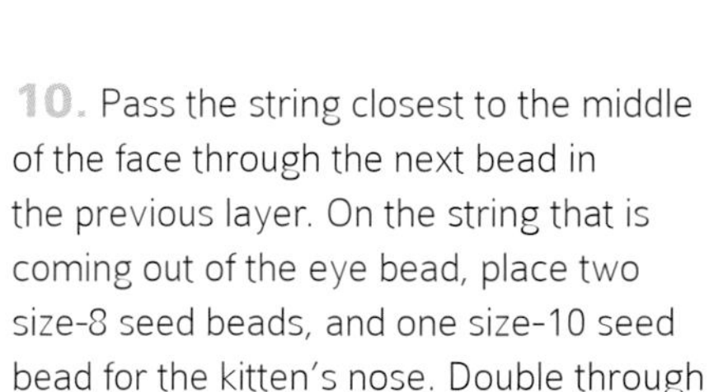

10. Pass the string closest to the middle of the face through the next bead in the previous layer. On the string that is coming out of the eye bead, place two size-8 seed beads, and one size-10 seed bead for the kitten's nose. Double through the size-10 seed bead (the nose).

11. Pass the lower string through the next two seed beads from the previous layer. Follow the instructions carefully. Be sure you are separating the groups of two beads to better seal up the shape, or you will be left with something resembling a Chinese lantern.

12 & 13. Place two size-8 seed beads on the upper string. Double the other string through the second seed bead. Pass the lower string through the next two seed beads from the previous layer.

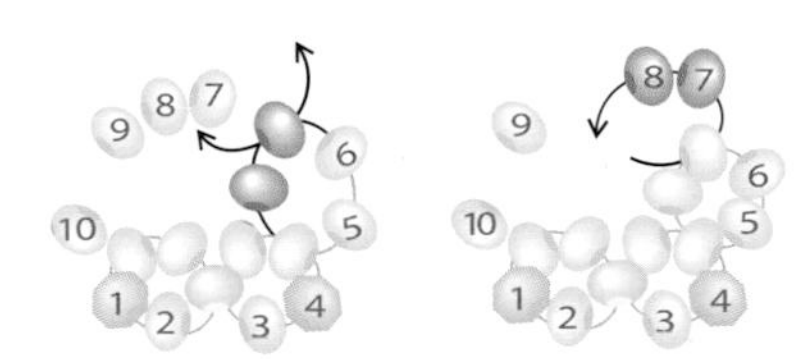

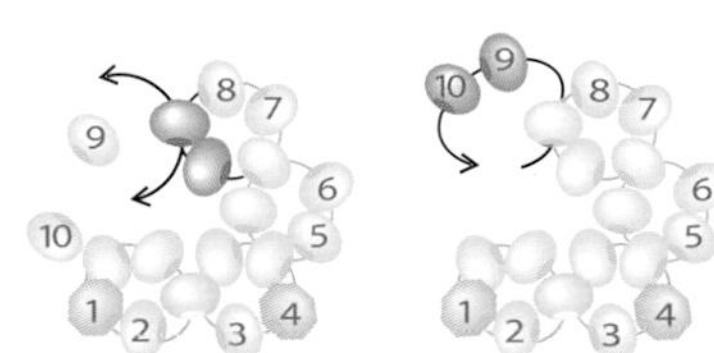

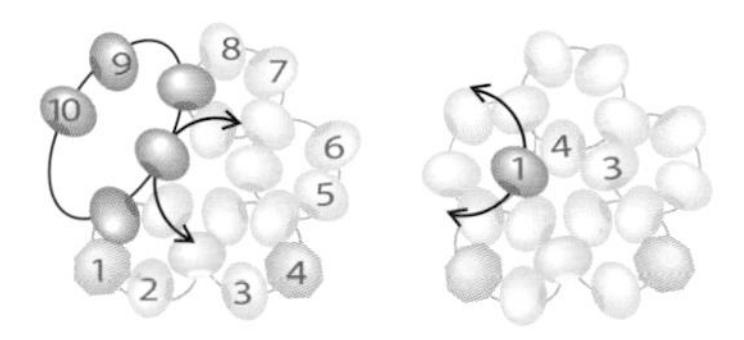

14. Place two size-8 seed beads on the upper string, then double the lower string through the second seed bead. Pass the lower string through the next two seed beads from the previous layer.

15. Place two size-8 seed beads on the upper string. Double the lower string through the second seed bead. Pass the lower string through the next two seed beads from the previous layer.

16. With the same string, continue to pass through the very first size-8 seed bead from the first panel of this layer. Double both strings through one size-8 seed bead On the string closest to the nose, place one size-8 seed bead.

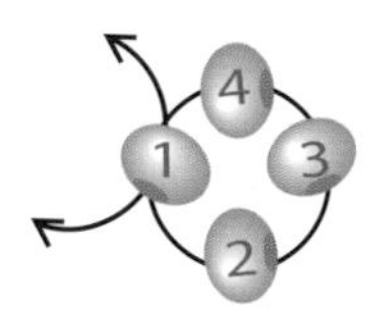

17. Pass through the next three seed beads from the previous row sitting in the topmost position. Both strings should be exiting the same bead from different sides.

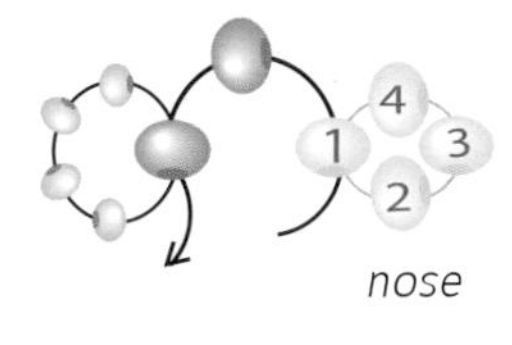

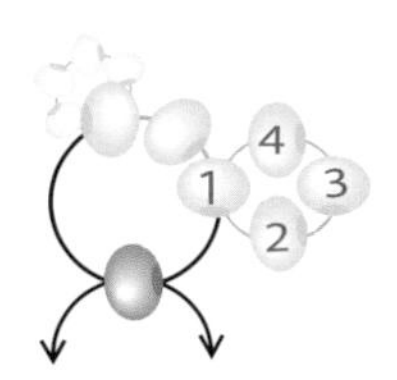

18. On the string furthest from the nose, place two size-8 seed beads and four size-10 seed beads for the toes. Double around and through the second size-8 seed bead. Double both strings through one size-8 seed bead.

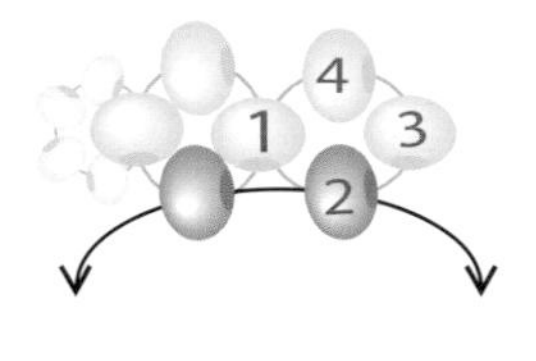

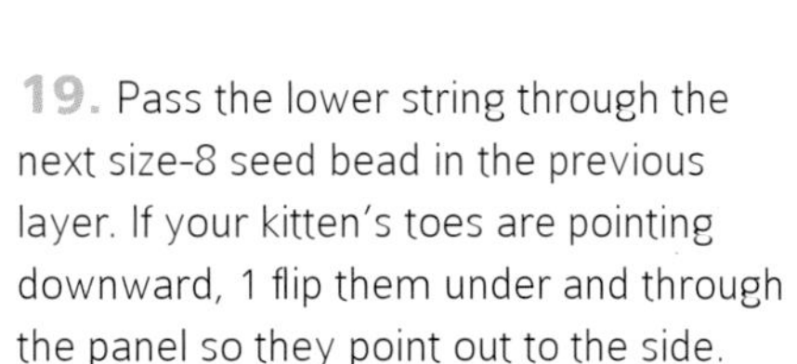

19. Pass the lower string through the next size-8 seed bead in the previous layer. If your kitten's toes are pointing downward, 1 flip them under and through the panel so they point out to the side.

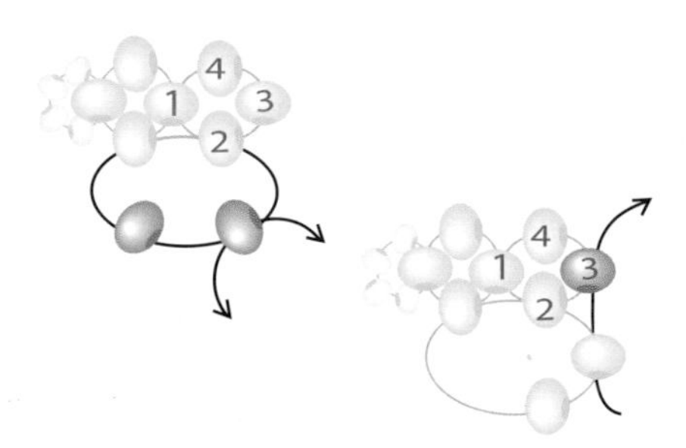

20. Place two size-8 seed beads on upper string. Double through the second size-8 seed bead. Pass the lower string through the next size-8 seed bead in the previous layer.

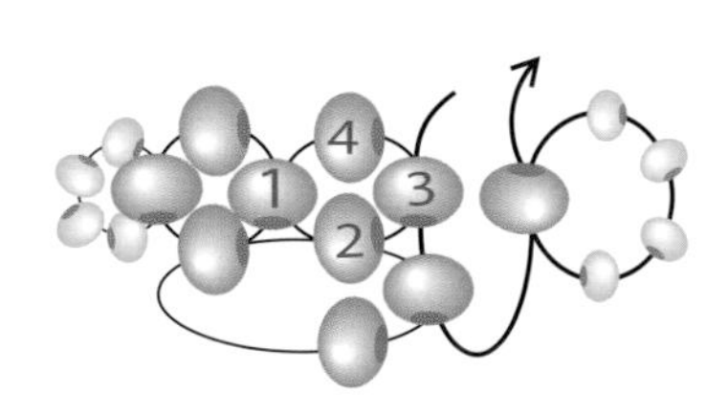

21. On the upper string, place one size-8 seed beads, and four size-10 seed beads for the kitten's other toes. Double around and through the size-8 seed bead. Double both strings through one size-8 seed bead.

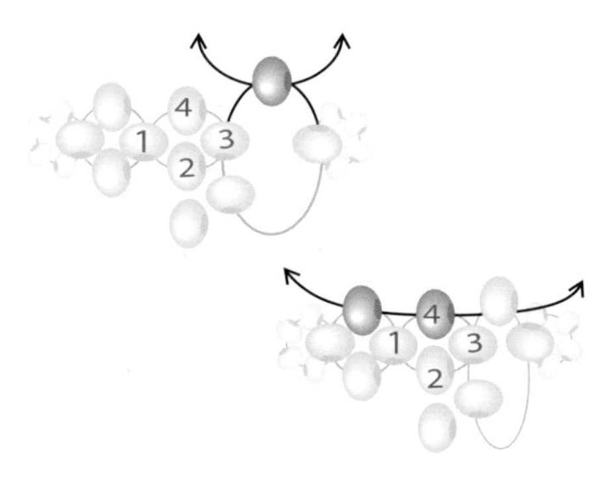

22. Pass the lower string through the closest size-8 seed bead in the previous layer, and the very first size-8 seed bead from the first panel 1of the kitten's body.

23, 24 & 25. On one string, place one size-8 seed bead, one size-10 seed bead, four size-8 seed beads, and one size-10 seed bead for the kitten's tail. Pass around the last size-10 seed bead, and back through the next four size-8 seed beads. Place one size-10 seed bead on the same string. Double around and through the first size-8 seed bead. Using two very tight knots, finish the string ends.

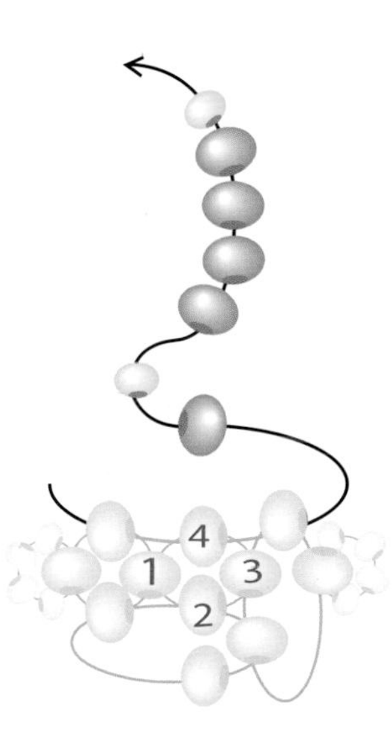

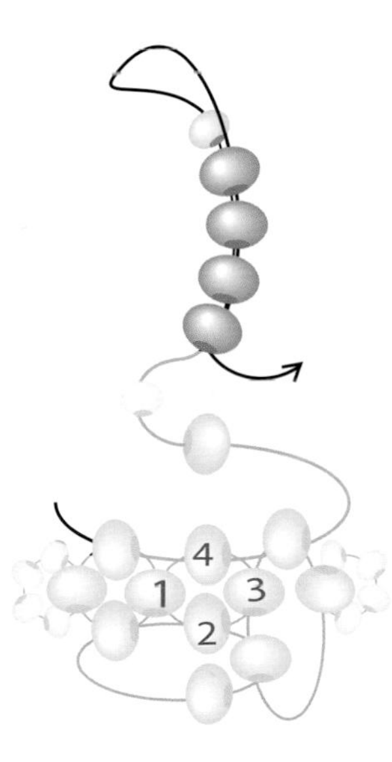

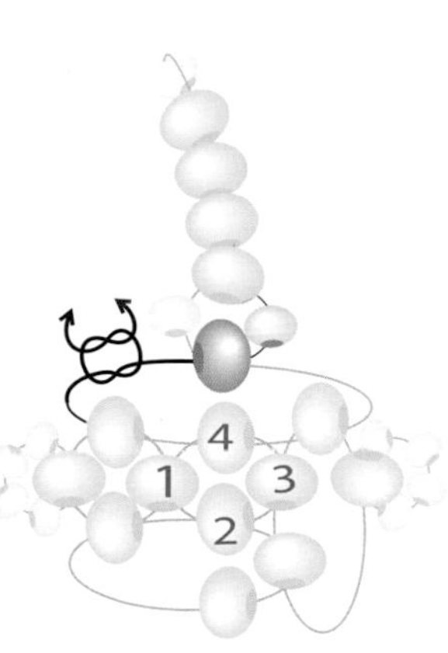